FLUFFY THE SPIDER'S HALLOWEEN SURPRISE

Juli Widjajanti

BLUEROSE PUBLISHERS
India | U.K.

Copyright © Juli Widjajanti 2024

All rights reserved by author. No part of this publication may be reproduced, stored in a retrieval system or transmitted in any form or by any means, electronic, mechanical, photocopying, recording or otherwise, without the prior permission of the author. Although every precaution has been taken to verify the accuracy of the information contained herein, the publisher assumes no responsibility for any errors or omissions. No liability is assumed for damages that may result from the use of information contained within.

BlueRose Publishers takes no responsibility for any damages, losses, or liabilities that may arise from the use or misuse of the information, products, or services provided in this publication.

For permissions requests or inquiries regarding this publication,
please contact:

BLUEROSE PUBLISHERS
www.BlueRoseONE.com
info@bluerosepublishers.com
+91 8882 898 898
+4407342408967

ISBN: 978-93-6783-474-9

Cover Design: Aman Sharma
Typesetting: Pooja Sharma

First Edition: December 2024

On a winter afternoon, a tiny spider named Fluffy shivered from the cold outside. "Brrrr! Where is the nearest cosy place?" he wondered. His little legs trembling like jelly.

Suddenly, he spotted an open window at one of the houses across from the tree he lived in. He peeked through and saw a warm and inviting room! "Aha! This looks like the perfect place to hang my coat... or, um, my web!"

Fluffy wasted no time! He hurried up to a cosy corner on the ceiling and spun the most intricate web you could imagine. "This is no ordinary web; it's my 'Fabulous silky Palace'!"

As the evening fell, he saw there were other spiders in the room across from his web. "Hello, he said!" He waved and waved, but they did not say anything. "Ah, they must be asleep" he said.

He continued to explore the room admiring the many books, toys and cosy corners he could imagine moving into next time.

He lowered himself onto the table and saw children dressed in white ghostly costumes with red eyes popping out, making them look terrifying.

One of the children noticed him and said, "Look at that fluffy-looking spider. It has no hat on." He thought Fluffy was one of the plastic spiders they had for Halloween. "It must had fallen off its head, he said!" The children laughed. Then he picked one of tiny hats and put it on Fluffy's head.

Fluffy felt the weight of the hat and lost his balance. He tipped to one side and then to the other side. The children laughed as they watched him move side to side.

Fluffy grinned, seeing the children laugh. He was happy that the children enjoy his company.

The girl stroked him gently and put him in her palm. He felt ticklish and shivered uncontrollably. It made her laugh.

"Time to trick-or-treat!" the boy said. The girl gently placed Fluffy on her right shoulder and said, "I'll take the spider with me". Fluffy's heart raced with excitement. He was going on his first trick-or-treat with his new friends.

They ventured from house to house, collecting sweets, bumping into other children and scaring each other with their ghostly walk. They squealed with delight, and the air filled with laughter and excitement.

Fluffy laughed with delight. He bumped into so many spiders and waved at them. "Happy Halloween, folks"! he exclaimed, dancing excitedly and spreading joy wherever he went.

After collecting sweets, they returned to their home happily. They settled in the bedroom and shared their adventure and laughter. The girl placed Fluffy gently on the table next to their beds. She smiled at him and patted him on the head.

Fluffy, buzzing with happiness, smiled widely. Halloween was more than just costumes and candy; it was about friends, laughter, and creating magical moments together. As the night ended, Fluffy whispered, "I can't wait for next Halloween!". His heart swelled with joy at the thought of all the adventures that awaited him next year.

Once the children were asleep, Fluffy left the room and snuggled in his cosy web. As he settled in, he drifted off to sleep, dreaming of all the fun adventures and delightful moments that awaited him next year.

www.ingramcontent.com/pod-product-compliance
Lightning Source LLC
LaVergne TN
LVHW061627070526
838199LV00070B/6616